The MINI FOOD PROCESSOR COOKBOOK

IRENA CHALMERS WITH RICKI OLDER

PENGUIN BOOKS

RFH

PENGUIN BOOKS

Published by the Penguin Group
Viking Penguin Inc., 40 West 23rd Street, New York, New York 10010, U.S.A.
Penguin Books Ltd, 27 Wrights Lane, London W8 5TZ, England
Penguin Books Australia Ltd, Ringwood, Victoria, Australia
Penguin Books Canada Ltd, 2801 John Street, Markham, Ontario, Canada L3R 1B4
Penguin Books (N.Z.) Ltd, 182–190 Wairau Road, Auckland 10, New Zealand
Penguin Books Ltd, Registered Offices: Harmondsworth, Middlesex, England

First published in Penguin Books 1988
Published simultaneously in Canada

Chalmers, Irena.
The mini food processor cookbook / Irena Chalmers with Ricki Older.
p.   cm.
1. Food processor cookery.   I. Older, Ricki.   II. Title.
TX840.F6C47   1988   88-2406
641'.5'89—dc19   CIP

Printed in Canada by Concept Com Inc.
Typeset by Pica Graphics

Editor Pamela Mitchell

Picture Editor Ilene Cherna Bellovin

CONTENTS

INTRODUCTION
How a Mini Food Processor Works

APPETIZERS 10

SOUPS 22

BEVERAGES 34

MEGA-MUFFINS & MINI-LOAVES 44

SALADS & VEGETABLES 54

Cauliflower Mousse	Pureed Vegetables	Stir-Fried Vegetables
Coleslaw	Sautéed Red Cabbage	Stuffed Green Peppers
Cucumber Salad	Spinach & Artichoke au Gratin	Stuffed Tomatoes
Potatoes au Gratin		Sweet Potato Crisp

SAUCES & DRESSING 68

Creamy Blue Cheese Dressing	Mayonnaise	Parmesan Cream Sauce
Fresh Basil Dressing	Mexican Salsa	Pesto
Fresh Tomato Sauce	Oil & Vinegar Dressing	Special Sauce for Artichokes

DESSERTS 78

COOKIES

Almond-Coconut Squares	Lemon Cookies
Chocolate Chip Cookies	Pecan Layer Bars

SAUCES

Apple-Cinnamon Sauce

Butterscotch Sauce

Hot Fudge Sauce

OTHER DESSERTS

Cheesecake with Graham Cracker Crust	Fresh Fruit Sorbets
Chocolate Mousse	One-Crust Pastry Shell
Dessert Crêpes	Pumpkin Chiffon Pie

INTRODUCTION

It is more than a dozen years since Carl Sontheimer changed the way millions of Americans prepare their meals. He is the genius who introduced us to the food processor and his marvelous machine was an immediate and astounding success. In the early days, we could measure our prestige in our neighborhood on the strength of whether we yet owned a Cuisinart. A food processor was high on everyone's birthday, Christmas, and anytime gift list. We all wanted one, and as the years went by, other manufacturers joined Cuisinarts, competing to fulfill our fantasies.

But all that was way back when we were trying to impress our friends with homemade Hollandaise sauce, steak tartare, or carrot cake. Remember that far-off time when our idea of a splendid dinner was shrimp cocktail, a large and luscious T-bone, and rich, dark chocolate mousse topped with a rosette of whipped cream?

A lot has changed since those heady, butter-drenched days. Things keep getting smaller: our families, our cars, our kitchens—even our appliances have become nuggetized. Microwave ovens are being manufactured in pint-size. Coffee pots, mixers, and toasters have levitated from the countertop and now nestle beneath our kitchen cabinets. We can indulge ourselves with homemade ice cream that is ready to eat from idea to reality in twenty minutes. And we are eating littlemeals!

Fortunately, confronted with constant change, some things do not change at all. We who love to eat good things *could*, if we chose to, eat mostly away from home or regularly buy take-out food to bring back with us, but we don't. We know the joys of preparing our own food at home—for it is only then that we can eat exactly *what* we want to eat, precisely *when* we want to eat it. And it is only then that the food, like the littlest bear's bowl of porridge, tastes just right.

Enter the mini food processor. This little darling will soon become as indispensable as the alarm clock. It is as practical and useful for someone who cooks a lot or hardly at all, and it will obediently perform simple but boring tasks—such as chopping a clove or two of garlic, cutting a cucumber into heartrendingly thin, even slices, or shredding the cabbage for coleslaw.

Just as the pocket calculator has made it unnecessary for us to know how to add or divide or multiply in order to balance our checkbooks, we no longer need a diploma or years of acquired skills to make homemade mayonnaise, two muffins, four popovers, six dessert crêpes, a fresh basil-scented pesto for a pot of pasta, or a bowl of guacamole to greet a guest. All we need is a mini food processor and a road map.

This book is a road map to get you started on your journey. You will soon find yourself using your mini food processor as frequently as you turn on the heat to make a cup of tea or coffee.

The mighty mini will mince up time and save the energy spent in chopping, slicing, pureeing, grating, and shredding. It will baby both you and your baby. It will add a whole new dimension to your dining pleasure.

To make this book as useful as possible, we have tested all of the recipes in a variety of mini, or compact, processors. So no matter what brand of processor you own, you can be sure that the recipe will work for you.

The term "on/off turns" was chosen as a good overall description of short uses of power. This means the same as "pulse," which is a word that some manufacturers use to describe this technique. Every mini processor turns on by the use of an interlocking cover and/or a switch or button. You can be sure that the capacity of the mini processor you own will not be exceeded by these recipes and you may find, after trying a recipe once, that you can make it in even larger quantities than are called for here.

The chart below suggests some general guidelines to follow in operating each function of the mini food processor. And while the chopping blade accounts for approximately 75 percent of the work done by a mini, don't ignore the slicing and shredding discs, which offer a number of creative and useful processing alternatives.

CHOPPING BLADE

For best results, cut foods into several evenly sized pieces; an onion, for example, should be cut into quarters. Fill the work bowl no more than half full for even chopping, as well as to prevent liquid mixtures from leaking out over the side of the work bowl.

To Blend/Puree: For safety's sake, food may be hot but should never be boiling. Use several on/off turns to chop food into smaller pieces. With the machine on, add liquids through the opening in the work bowl cover. Process until smooth. Recommended for dips, flavored butters, salad dressings, sauces, spreads, milk shakes, baby foods, etc.
Foods: Fresh, cooked, or canned fruits and vegetables, cooked meats, cooked cereal grains, butter, ice cream, soft cheeses.

To Chop: Use on/off turns of no more than 1 to 2 seconds for consistent evenness. Continue to use on/off turns until chopped to the desired size. Foods may be chopped even after they've been added to other ingredients, such as nuts in a cheese spread or a muffin mix.
Foods: Cheese, fruits, hard-cooked eggs, nuts, olives, pickles, vegetables; raw and cooked fish, meat, or poultry.

To Crumb/Grate: Use on/off turns to chop into smaller pieces, then process to desired consistency.
Foods: Chocolate, citrus rind (preferably with some sugar from the recipe), cookies, crackers, hard cheeses such as Parmesan or Romano, stale or fresh bread.

To Mince: Both the work bowl and the food to be minced should be as clean and dry as possible. Cut longer foods, such as scallions or chives, into shorter pieces. Use on/off turns until minced to desired consistency. Scrape down the sides of the work bowl occasionally.
Foods: Fresh herbs, garlic, ginger, parsley, shallots, scallions.

To Mix: Use short on/off turns just to blend the ingredients. Do not overprocess! Quick breads, muffins, and cookies are adequately mixed even if a trace of flour remains visible in the dough.
Foods: Cookie doughs, custards, muffins, pastry, pizza dough, puddings, quick breads.

SLICING DISC

For best results, large foods should be cut to fit into the feed tube but not extend higher than its top. Cut large foods in half horizontally and even off one end, placing this side down on the slicing disc. Cut slender foods into short lengths and pack them fairly tightly in the feed tube. Different-sized slices result from slicing foods upright or on their sides; for example, upright carrots produce small round circles and horizontal carrots produce long thin strips.

Chill cooked meat and firm cheeses such as cheddar before slicing. However, if you can't pierce a piece of food with the tip of a knife, it will be too firm for the mini processor.

Be ready to exert pressure on the pusher before engaging the machine. Match the pressure on the pusher to the firmness of the food being sliced.

Foods: Moderately firm fresh fruits and vegetables such as apples, bananas, beans, beets, carrots, celery, cucumbers, lemons, limes, mushrooms, onions, oranges, peppers, potatoes, squash, strawberries; well-chilled cooked meat; firm cheeses such as Swiss and cheddar.

SHREDDING DISC

For best results, large foods should be cut to fit into the feed tube but not extend higher than its top. Chill soft cheeses such as Monterey jack, Muenster, and mozzarella for 10 to 20 minutes in the freezer to process easily. Chill hard cheeses such as cheddar, Swiss, gouda, and colby in the refrigerator.

Shreds of different lengths result from shredding foods upright or on their sides. For example, upright zucchini produces short shreds while horizontal zucchini produces long shreds.

Match the pressure on the pusher to the firmness of the food being shredded. Always use a light pressure on the pusher when shredding cheeses.
Foods: Moderately firm fresh fruits and vegetables such as apples, beets, carrots, cucumbers, jicama, pears, potatoes, radishes, squash, zucchini; cheeses as discussed; pickles.

APPETIZERS

GARDEN PATCH DIP

Vegetables fresh from Mr. McGregor's garden are finely chopped, made fragrant with sweet basil, and mixed with sour cream. Into this melange can be dipped a colorful assortment of baby vegetables, tortilla chips, or slender Italian breadsticks. A nasturtium blossom or a pansy makes a charming, whimsical decoration for the bowl.

Makes 1½ cups

6 or more fresh basil leaves, or substitute any other fresh herb

2 scallions, cut in pieces

½ small carrot, cut in pieces

½ small green pepper, cut in pieces

1 cup sour cream

Insert the chopping blade and add the basil. Use on/off turns until minced. Add the vegetables to the work bowl. Use 3 to 4 on/off turns to chop. Stir the mixture into the sour cream. Chill and serve.

GUACAMOLE

A great guacamole gridlock has gripped the land. Everyone, it seems, adores guacamole. Here are two tips for success: Use really ripe avocados. (If you enclose the avocados in a brown paper bag along with a banana, the ethylene gas given off as the banana matures hastens the ripening of the avocados, too.) To prevent the guacamole from darkening, cover the surface with a thin film of sour cream, yogurt, or mayonnaise.

Makes 1½ cups

1 clove garlic

½ small onion

2 medium-size ripe avocados

1 teaspoon fresh lime or lemon juice

1 small tomato, quartered

Salt and pepper

Tabasco sauce (optional)

Insert the chopping blade and add the garlic and onion. Use on/off turns until finely minced. Add the avocados and lime juice. Use on/off turns until the avocado is well blended. Scrape down the work bowl sides as needed. Add the tomato and use 3 on/off turns to chop. Season to taste. Add Tabasco sauce if you like a spicier flavor.

HERB PUFFS

The mini processor makes easy work of beating eggs into cream puff
paste. These puffs are delightful served warm as they are or as a casing
for any savory filling you can conjure up. Cut open and fill with
cream cheese and caviar, Guacamole (page 11), or any other stuffing
that will be firm enough to hold its shape and not drip down a tie,
an arm, or a cleavage.

Makes 23–30 small puffs

Preheat the oven to 400 degrees

¼ cup fresh herbs, such as basil,
tarragon, dill, rosemary, thyme, or a
combination

½ cup water

3 tablespoons butter, cut into pieces

½ cup flour

2 eggs

Insert the chopping blade and add the herbs. Use 6 to 8 on/off turns until the herbs are finely minced.

Bring the water and butter to a rolling boil in a medium-sized saucepan, regulating the heat so that the butter is melted at the moment the water reaches the boiling point. Stir in the flour all at once. Reduce the heat to low and continue stirring vigorously for 1 minute. (The timing is important because overcooking this mixture will prevent the puffs from rising in the oven.) Remove from the heat. Add the mixture to the herbs in the work bowl. Add the eggs and use 16 to 18 on/off turns to incorporate completely (the mixture will become thick and shiny). The dough should hold its shape when lifted with a spoon.

Drop by scant teaspoonfuls onto an unbuttered baking sheet. Bake in the preheated oven for 10 minutes. Reduce the heat to 375 degrees and bake for 15 minutes longer. Cool the puffs away from drafts.

SHRIMP COCKTAIL SAUCE

Use the smaller amount of horseradish first and add more until it reaches the desired "bite" level. A grapefruit spoon easily scoops out the seeds from each tomato and the mini processor chops the tomatoes so finely that there is no need to peel them. Try the sauce also with chilled, cooked crab meat or fresh oysters.

Makes 1½ cups

¼ **small onion**

6 **plum tomatoes, halved and seeded**

2 **tablespoons fresh lemon juice**

2-3 **tablespoons prepared horseradish**

2 **tablespoons tomato paste**

2 **teaspoons Worcestershire sauce**

Insert the chopping blade and add the onion. Use 3 to 4 on/off turns to finely mince the onion. Add the remaining ingredients and use on/off turns until well combined and smooth. Chill and serve.

SHRIMP SPREAD

This is one of those always-useful recipes because you can substitute a 4½-ounce can of shrimp for the fresh shrimp and have all the ingredients in the kitchen cupboard. (Keep a party loaf of rye bread in the freezer and you will be prepared for almost all of life's small crises.)

Serves 24

Preheat the broiler

1 small scallion, cut in 2-inch lengths

⅓ cup Mayonnaise (page 72)

½ teaspoon prepared mustard

8–10 drops Tabasco sauce

6–8 pitted jumbo black olives

1 cup cooked small shrimp

Party rye bread

Insert the chopping blade and add the scallion. Use on/off turns to process until minced. Add the mayonnaise, mustard, Tabasco sauce, and black olives. Use 3 on/off turns to blend; add the shrimp and use 4 to 5 on/off turns until the shrimp and olives are chopped. Spread on the rye slices and broil for 3 to 4 minutes or until browned and puffed. Serve hot.

If you prefer, you can serve it cold, spread on crackers, as a filling for hollowed-out cherry tomatoes, or mounded on wedges of green and red pepper or on cucumber, zucchini, or carrot circles.

SMOKED TROUT MOUSSE

For a very grand presentation, put an additional whole smoked trout in the center of the serving tray and arrange cucumber slices topped with the mousse around the edge.

Serves 12

1 small onion, halved

1 whole smoked trout (about 6 ounces), skinned and boned

3 ounces cream cheese

1 tablespoon fresh lemon juice

Dash Tabasco sauce

Cucumber slices

Lemon wedges

Parsley

Insert the chopping blade and add the onion. Use 2 to 3 on/off turns to chop. Add the trout, cream cheese, lemon juice, and Tabasco sauce. Process until a smooth puree has formed.

Mound the trout mousse on the cucumber slices. Arrange on a serving tray, garnished with the lemon wedges and parsley.

STUFFED MUSHROOMS

Try to find uniformly sized small mushrooms. Guests at cocktail parties will often refuse anything larger than one-bite size.

Serves 24–30

Preheat the oven to 350 degrees

2 scallions

4 ounces Monterey Jack or mozzarella cheese, cut in 4 pieces

½ pound mild Italian sausage

24–30 mushrooms, wiped clean, stems removed

Insert the chopping blade and add the scallions. Use on/off turns to process until minced. Add the cheese to the work bowl and use on/off turns until chopped; remove the scallions and cheese to a mixing bowl.

Remove the sausage casing, if necessary, and brown the meat in a skillet. Drain on paper towels. Put the sausage meat in the work bowl and use 6 to 8 on/off turns until it is coarsely chopped. Add to the scallions and cheese and blend.

Fill the mushrooms with about 1 teaspoon of the sausage-and-cheese mixture. Arrange the mushrooms in a buttered 10-by-15-inch baking pan. Bake, uncovered, in the preheated oven for 25 minutes. Serve hot.

SWISS CHEESE FONDUE

Here is an old and beloved favorite, making a welcome comeback. In Switzerland, the folks like to serve fondue with small boiled potatoes, a bowl of cornichons or other small pickles, and sometimes even with cubes of ham. I like also to have a cluster of radishes with coarse salt near at hand.

Makes 3½–4 cups

1 clove garlic

¾ cup white wine

¼ cup water

½ teaspoon Worcestershire sauce

½ teaspoon dry mustard

1 pound Swiss cheese

3 tablespoons flour

Loaf of French bread

Insert the chopping blade, add the garlic, and use on/off turns to process until minced. Combine the garlic, wine, water, and seasonings in a large saucepan; heat until simmering.

Cut the cheese into pieces to fit the feed tube. Insert the shredding disc and lightly process the cheese. Toss the cheese with the flour in a large bowl. Add this to the hot wine mixture in the pan and continue to heat until melted, stirring occasionally. Dip cubes of crisp French bread into the hot fondue.

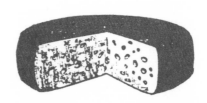

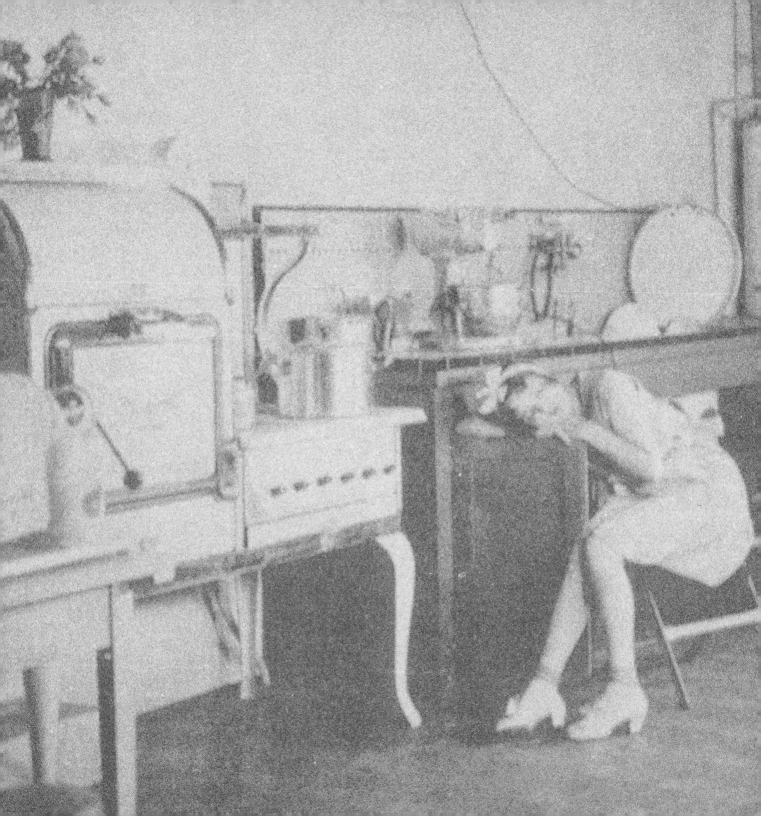

WALNUT-COATED CHEESE BALL

An almost instantly made hors d'oeuvre, the cheese ball is always popular.

Makes 1½ cups

½ **cup parsley leaves**

⅓ **cup walnuts, toasted**

1 clove garlic

4 ounces sharp cheddar cheese, cut in pieces

6 ounces cream cheese, cut in pieces

1 teaspoon Worcestershire sauce

Insert the chopping blade and add the parsley. Use on/off turns to chop. Add the walnuts and use 4 on/off turns to finely chop. Set aside. Place the garlic in the work bowl and use on/off turns until finely chopped. Add the cheddar cheese; use 6 to 8 on/off turns to chop the cheese. Add the cream cheese and Worcestershire sauce and use 10 to 15 on/off turns to combine all of the ingredients. Scrape down the sides of the work bowl.

Spread the parsley and walnut mixture out onto a sheet of wax paper. Form the cheese into a ball and roll it in the mixture to coat. Wrap the ball up in the wax paper and chill it in the refrigerator for 1 or 2 hours until firm. Serve at room temperature with crisp crackers or sliced vegetables.

SOUPS

CANADIAN CHEDDAR CHEESE SOUP

A comforting and easily prepared soup for a cold winter's night.

Serves 4

1 small onion

1 stalk celery, cut in 2-inch pieces

3 cups chicken broth

¼ cup cornstarch

⅛ teaspoon paprika

⅛ teaspoon cayenne pepper

Salt

6 ounces sharp cheddar cheese, well chilled

1 small carrot, peeled and cut in 4 even pieces

2 tablespoons butter

Minced parsley

Cooked bacon, crumbled

Insert the chopping blade and add the onion and celery. Use 2 to 3 on/off turns to chop. Set aside. Add 1 cup of the chicken broth, the cornstarch, and the seasonings to the work bowl. Blend for 2 seconds. Set aside.

Insert the shredding disc. Cut the cheddar cheese in pieces to fit the feed tube. Process, using a light pressure. Set aside. Stand the carrot pieces in the feed tube and process, using medium pressure. Add to the onion and celery.

Melt the butter in a large saucepan; add all of the vegetables and cook over low heat until the onion is tender. Add the remaining 2 cups chicken broth to the saucepan. Cook over moderate heat until thickened. Add the cheese and stir over moderate heat until melted and the soup is heated through. Adjust the seasonings.

Garnish with the parsley and bacon.

CREAM OF WATERCRESS SOUP

Any leftover cooked vegetable (such as broccoli, zucchini, carrot, cauliflower, spinach, mushroom, or celery) can be used to make a variation of this soup. Chop the leftover vegetables, cook the onions and celery as directed, add the prepared vegetables, and proceed.

Serves 2

2 cups watercress leaves

1 small onion, halved

1 stalk celery, cut in pieces

2 tablespoons butter

¼ cup water

2 tablespoons flour

2¼ cups chicken broth

Salt and black pepper

Insert the chopping blade and add the watercress. Use 2 on/off turns to chop. Add the onion and celery and use 3 on/off turns to chop.

Melt the butter in a medium-sized saucepan. Add the vegetables and ¼ cup water. Cook over medium-low heat for about 10 minutes or until the vegetables have softened.

Insert the chopping blade and place the flour and 1 cup of the chicken broth in the work bowl. Process for 2 seconds. Add to the saucepan with the remaining broth and season to taste with salt and pepper. Bring to a boil, stirring occasionally. Reduce the heat and simmer gently for 5 minutes.

CREAMY POTATO SOUP

This comforting, most basic of all soups may be varied by adventurous cooks: Substitute an apple or a winter pear or even a cup of pureed pumpkin for one of the potatoes. For a garnish, try adding a scattering of chopped chives, crumbled bacon, or shredded cheddar cheese.

Serves 4

1 stalk celery, cut in 4 even pieces

1 medium-size onion, halved

3 medium-size potatoes, peeled and quartered

2 tablespoons butter

3 cups chicken broth

1–2 sprigs fresh dill, or ½ teaspoon dried dill

1 cup milk

1 teaspoon oregano

Salt and white pepper

Insert the slicing disc and put the celery pieces in the feed tube. Slice, using medium pressure. Repeat with the onion halves and then the potato quarters.

Melt the butter in a large saucepan. Add the celery and onion and cook for 5 minutes. Add the potatoes and the chicken broth and bring to a boil. Reduce the heat, cover, and simmer for 25 to 30 minutes or until the potatoes are tender. Cool for about 10 minutes.

Insert the chopping blade and add the dill. Use on/off turns until minced. Ladle the work bowl half full of the soup mixture. Use 6 to 8 on/off turns to puree the potatoes, then pour the mixture into a bowl. Repeat with the remaining soup. Return all of the pureed soup to the saucepan and add the milk and oregano. Season to taste with salt and pepper, heat through, and serve.

FRENCH ONION SOUP

This classic soup has all the work removed when the mini processor slices all the onions for you in a few seconds. Treat yourself to freshly grated Parmesan and the best Swiss cheese you can find to add incomparable flavor to the soup. Cut the Parmesan cheese into small pieces, insert the chopping blade, and use on/off turns until grated. With the shredding disc inserted, cut the Swiss cheese into pieces to fit the feed tube and process.

Serves 4

3 medium-size onions, halved lengthwise

4 tablespoons butter

4 cups beef broth

4 slices toasted French bread

4 ounces Swiss cheese, grated

2 ounces Parmesan cheese, grated

Insert the slicing disc. Place an onion half in the feed tube and slice, using medium pressure. Continue with the remaining onions.

Melt the butter in a large covered saucepan, add the onions, and cook over low heat for about 30 minutes, stirring occasionally (cooking the onions slowly preserves their natural sweetness). Add the beef broth and bring to a boil. Reduce the heat, cover, and simmer for about 30 minutes.

Preheat the broiler. Pour the soup into 4 ovenproof bowls, add 1 toasted French bread slice to each, and cover each evenly with both the Swiss and Parmesan cheeses. Place under the broiler and cook until the cheese is bubbling hot and just starting to brown. Serve at once.

GAZPACHO

The mini processor chops the preparation time for making this splendid cold Spanish vegetable soup down to a few seconds.

Serves 4

1 clove garlic

8 fresh basil leaves

8–10 sprigs fresh chives

2 medium-size ripe tomatoes, seeded and quartered

¾ cup tomato juice or V8 juice

½ medium-size cucumber, peeled, seeded, and quartered

½ medium-size green pepper, seeded and quartered

½ small onion, halved

1 tablespoon wine vinegar

2 tablespoons olive oil

Salt and pepper

Insert the chopping blade, add the garlic, and process until minced. Add the fresh herbs and use on/off turns to process until minced. Add the tomatoes and tomato juice and process until finely chopped. Set aside in a storage container. Place the remaining ingredients in the work bowl and process until the vegetables are finely chopped. Combine thoroughly with the tomato mixture. Chill for several hours until serving time.

MUSHROOM-BARLEY SOUP

This soup makes its own stock while it cooks — a real time-saver and a flavor bonus. In place of chicken, you may substitute turkey portions, which are now so readily available in supermarkets. The choice of light or dark meat is up to you.

Serves 4

8 medium-size mushrooms

1 medium-size carrot, peeled and cut in even lengths

1 stalk celery, cut in even lengths

1 medium-size onion, halved

5 cups water

¾ pound chicken breasts or thighs, skin and excess fat removed

1 bay leaf

¼ cup barley

1½ teaspoons salt

1 teaspoon pepper

Separate the mushroom stems and caps. Insert the slicing disc. Place the mushroom caps on their sides in the feed tube and slice, using medium pressure. Slice the mushroom stems in the same manner; set aside. Stand the carrot and celery lengths on end in the feed tube, and slice, using medium pressure. Slice the onion halves, using medium pressure.

Place all of the ingredients in a large saucepan and bring to a boil. Reduce the heat, cover, and simmer for 1 hour. Remove the chicken pieces and let cool slightly. Use a fork to shred the meat; discard any bones. Return the meat to the saucepan. Adjust the seasonings. Heat through and serve.

PEA SOUP

Having homemade pea soup makes a house into a home. Add a meaty ham bone for additional flavor. After cooking, remove any meat from the bone, discard the bone, and add the meat to the soup. This recipe can be cut in half and it also freezes well.

Serves 4

2 cups dried split peas

2 quarts water

3 stalks celery, quartered

1 medium-size onion, quartered

1 small carrot, peeled and quartered

2 bay leaves

Pinch thyme

Salt and white pepper

1 cup croutons

Combine the peas and water in a large pot; bring to a boil and then simmer gently for 5 minutes. Remove from the heat, cover, and let stand for 1 hour or overnight.

Insert the chopping blade and add the celery, onion, and carrot. Use 4 to 5 on/off turns to chop the vegetables. Add to the soup with the bay leaves and thyme. Bring to a boil and then reduce the heat to a simmer. (If you are using a ham bone, add it at this point.) Cook for 2½ to 3 hours or until the peas are very soft. If necessary, thin with water to desired consistency. Season to taste with salt and pepper, then heat through and serve, garnished with croutons.

TOMATO SOUP

One of the greatest advances in civilization in this century is the availability of basil and other fresh herbs. Those who search diligently will surely find their efforts rewarded.

Serves 4

10–12 fresh basil leaves or 1½ teaspoons dried basil

1 small onion, quartered

2 tablespoons butter

4 medium-size tomatoes, quartered

2 cups chicken broth

Salt and pepper

½ cup heavy cream (optional)

Insert the chopping blade, add the basil, and use 6 to 8 on/off turns to mince finely. Add the onion and use 2 to 3 on/off turns to chop.

Melt the butter in a large saucepan and add the basil and onion. Cook over moderate heat for 5 to 7 minutes or until the onions are soft. Add the tomatoes and the broth and bring to a boil. Reduce the heat, cover, and simmer 30 to 40 minutes. Cool slightly.

Ladle the work bowl half full of the tomato mixture. Use 6 to 8 on/off turns to puree until smooth. Return the mixture to the saucepan. Repeat the process with the remaining soup. Strain through a coarse sieve if you like a smoother texture, pressing down with the back of a spoon to extract all of the liquid. Return all of the soup to the saucepan, season to taste with salt and pepper, and heat through, adding the cream if you wish.

BEVERAGES

ALMOND-ORANGE CREAM

It has become popular of late to serve dessert in the form of an after-dinner drink with ice cream as the base. You can try this in various combinations with your choice of ice cream — coffee is a good bet — and liqueur (try Frangelico, Baileys Irish Cream, or Truffles Liqueur du Chocolat). One large scoop of ice cream is usually about ½ cup and measuring is not too critical in this recipe.

Serves 2

2 scoops vanilla ice cream

3 ounces almond-flavored liqueur

¼ cup fresh orange juice

Grated rind of 1 orange

Orange slices (optional)

Insert the chopping blade and add the ice cream. Use 3 on/off turns to soften. Add the remaining ingredients and process until the drink is smooth. Decorate with thin half-moon orange slices for a final flourish.

BANANA FROSTY

For a more intense banana flavor, add one more banana — you'll need to eat this drink with a spoon but banana lovers won't mind a bit!

Serves 1

1 medium-size ripe banana, quartered

2 scoops vanilla ice cream

⅛ teaspoon nutmeg or allspice

¾ cup milk

Insert the chopping blade and add the banana. Use 3 to 4 on/off turns to puree. Add the ice cream and use 6 to 8 on/off turns to break it up. Add the remaining ingredients and process until smooth. Serve immediately.

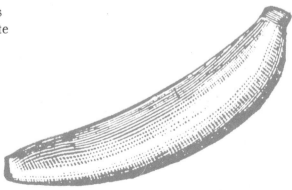

Breakfast Cocktail

*A portable breakfast that the mini processor
makes in moments. Fruit and egg are
quickly pureed and honey adds just the right
amount of sweetness. Banana, strawberry,
peach, orange, pear, or pineapple are
just a few of the fruits you might try.*

Serves 1

1 egg

⅔ cup chopped ripe fruit

1 cup milk

1 teaspoon honey

Insert the chopping
blade; add the egg and the fruit. Use 6 to 8
on/off turns to puree the fruit. Add the milk
and honey and use 2 on/off turns to combine.
Pour into a glass, drink, and go!

CALIFORNIA SANGRIA

The classic sangria is made with red wine but sometimes I like to use white in this recipe. A small chunk of peeled fresh pineapple, sliced along with the other fruits, is also a welcome addition to this drink. Add a little sparkle to each glass with chilled club soda.

Serves 4–6

1 750-ml. bottle dry red wine or fragrant white wine, such as a California Gewürztraminer, chilled

2 ounces brandy (a fruit brandy such as pear brandy is a sensational addition)

2 tablespoons sugar

1 firm orange, chilled

1 firm lemon, chilled

Berries or sliced fruits

Combine the wine, brandy, and sugar in a large pitcher. Cut off both ends of the orange and lemon, then halve lengthwise. Insert the slicing disc and place each fruit half in the feed tube. Slice, using medium pressure on the pusher. Repeat with the remaining fruit halves. Add the fruit slices to the pitcher. Chill 30 to 60 minutes. Serve with plenty of ice and float a cornucopia of berries and/or more sliced fruits in the wine.

CUCUMBER COOLER

The person who dreamed up this idea must surely have had an overabundance of cucumbers in the garden. The result is a cooling summer drink that will most certainly inspire you to create variations with other vegetables. If you have eight vegetables on hand, you could devise a drink and call it V8!

Serves 1

3 sprigs fresh dill, plus more for garnish

½ cucumber, unpeeled, seeded, and quartered

1 cup buttermilk

Salt and white pepper

Insert the chopping blade and add the 3 sprigs of dill. Use on/off turns until finely minced. Add the cucumber; use on/off turns until smooth. Add the buttermilk and process until smooth. Season to taste with salt and pepper. Garnish with fresh dill. Serve with a smoked salmon sandwich or other charismatic composition.

FRESH PLUM SHAKE

Here's a shake that calorie watchers will love. Use more or less honey depending on the sweetness of the plums. The touch of lemon juice makes a good counterpoint.

Serves 1

2 fresh plums, cut into pieces

⅔ **cup buttermilk**

2 teaspoons honey

1 teaspoon lemon juice

Insert the chopping blade and add all of the ingredients. Use several very short on/off turns until the plums are well chopped. The drink will have an attractive froth on the surface.

ORANGE JULIANA

Those who frequent the shopping malls of America will recognize this drink as their favorite refresher, an "Orange Julius." Crack the ice by putting the cubes in a plastic bag, holding it shut, and tapping with a heavy saucepan.

Serves 1

⅓ **cup frozen orange juice concentrate**

⅓ **cup milk**

⅓ **cup water**

¼ **teaspoon vanilla extract**

1 teaspoon sugar

2 ice cubes, cracked

Insert the chopping blade and add all of the ingredients. Use several very short on/off turns until the ingredients are well blended and frothy but some ice particles still remain.

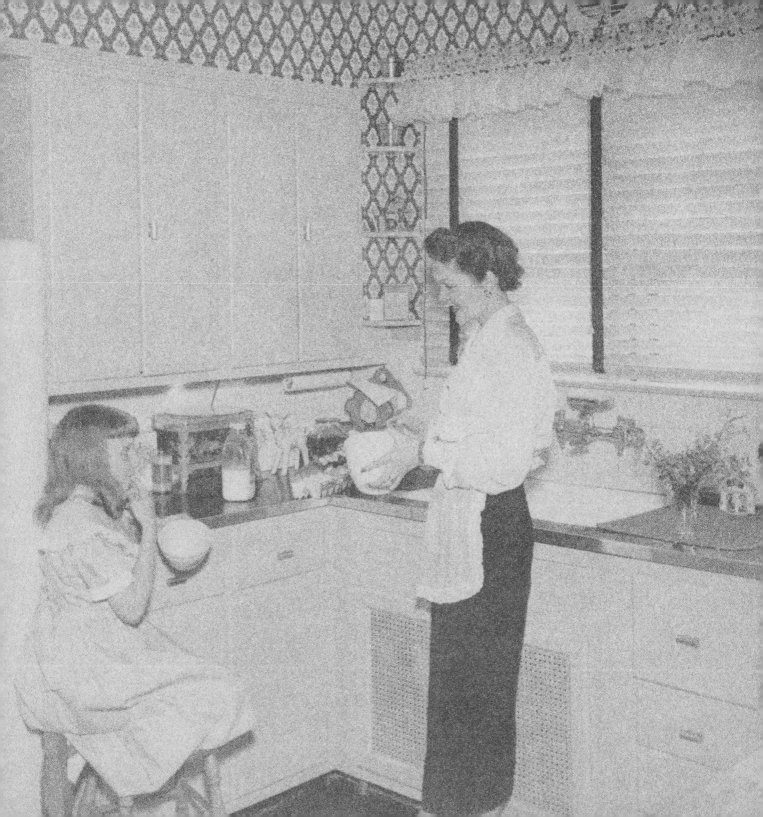

PEACH MILK SHAKE

Use one or two scoops of ice cream, depending on how thick you like your shakes. Brown sugar and cinnamon provide a mellow contrast to the fresh peach.

Serves 1

1 fresh ripe peach, peeled and pitted

1 teaspoon brown sugar

Dash cinnamon

1-2 scoops vanilla ice cream

¾ cup milk

Insert the chopping blade; add the peach, brown sugar, and cinnamon. Use 2 on/off turns to chop the peach. Add the ice cream; use 6 to 8 on/off turns to break up the ice cream. Add the milk and process until smooth. Serve quickly.

STRAWBERRY SMOOTHIE

Did you know that the smell of strawberries has a mildly tranquilizing effect? The Strawberry Smoothie will make you healthy and perhaps improve your disposition at the same time. Who could ask for anything more?

Serves 1

7 fresh, very ripe whole strawberries, stems removed

1 cup low-fat strawberry yogurt

¼ cup low-fat milk

¼ teaspoon vanilla extract

Sprig of fresh mint

Insert the chopping blade in the work bowl. Add 6 strawberries, the yogurt, milk, and vanilla and use on/off turns to process the mixture until smooth. Serve in an elegant tall glass, decorated with the remaining strawberry and the mint sprig.

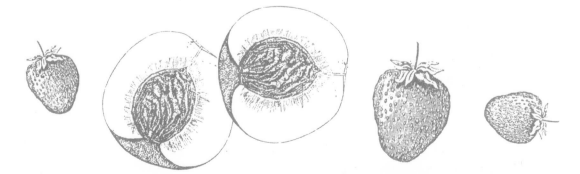

MEGA-MUFFINS & MINI-LOAVES

BRAN-RAISIN MUFFINS

Serve these muffins warm, accompanied by butter whipped with honey in the mini processor. Insert the chopping blade, use two parts butter to one part honey, and whip away.

Makes 6 standard muffins or 3 mega-muffins

Preheat the oven to 350 degrees

⅓ cup buttermilk

2 tablespoons melted butter

3 tablespoons molasses

1 egg

¾ teaspoon baking soda

⅔ cup whole wheat flour

½ cup bran cereal flakes

⅓ cup raisins

Insert the chopping blade and add the buttermilk, butter, molasses, egg, and baking soda. Use 3 on/off turns to combine. Add the flour and bran and use 3 on/off turns to combine. Remove the chopping blade and stir in the raisins.

Pour the batter evenly into 6 buttered standard muffin cups or 3 buttered 6-ounce custard cups. Bake for 15 to 20 minutes or until a tester inserted in the center comes out clean.

CARROT LOAF

Carrot cake survives all the food fashions and fads because it is so versatile. It serves as a mid-morning snack or as a dessert after dinner. It keeps wonderfully well too.

Makes one 5-by-2-inch loaf

Preheat the oven to 350 degrees

2 medium-size carrots, peeled

⅓ cup sugar

⅓ cup vegetable oil

1 egg

1 teaspoon cinnamon

1 teaspoon baking powder

½ teaspoon baking soda

Pinch salt

¾ cup flour

Insert the shredding disc. Cut the carrots in lengths to fit the feed tube horizontally and use medium pressure to shred on the horizontal (you should have ⅔ cup shredded carrot). Set aside.

Insert the chopping blade and add the sugar, oil, and egg. Process for 10 to 15 seconds or until the mixture is creamy. Add the cinnamon, baking powder, baking soda, and salt and use 2 on/off turns to combine. Add the flour and carrots and use 2 to 3 on/off turns to combine.

Pour the batter into a buttered mini-loaf pan. Bake for 30 to 35 minutes or until a toothpick inserted in the center comes out clean. Cool on a rack for 10 minutes before turning out of the pan.

CHOCOLATE CHIP MUFFINS

There is no law that says you can't have chocolate for breakfast.

Makes 6 standard muffins or 3 mega-muffins

Preheat the oven to 350 degrees

2 tablespoons sugar

2 tablespoons butter

1 egg

½ cup milk

1 teaspoon vanilla extract

1 teaspoon baking powder

1 cup flour

⅓ cup chocolate chips

Insert the chopping blade, add the sugar and butter, and use 6 to 8 on/off turns to cream the mixture. Add the egg, milk, vanilla, and baking powder. Use 2 to 3 on/off turns to combine. Add the flour and chocolate chips and use 2 on/off turns to combine.

Pour the batter evenly into 6 buttered standard muffin cups or 3 buttered 6-ounce custard cups. Bake in the preheated oven for 20 to 25 minutes.

These taste their very best served warm, when the chocolate is meltingly soft.

CRANBERRY-ORANGE MUFFINS

If you buy extra cranberries in November, you can keep them frozen and have this tart berry muffin all year long.

Makes 6 standard muffins or 3 mega-muffins

Preheat the oven to 350 degrees

6 tablespoons sugar

Rind and juice of ½ medium-size orange

1 tablespoon oil

1 egg

½ teaspoon baking powder

¼ teaspoon baking soda

1 cup flour

¾ cup whole fresh cranberries

Insert the chopping blade and add the sugar and orange rind. Process until finely minced. Add enough water to the orange juice to equal ⅓ cup. Add to the work bowl along with the oil, egg, baking powder, and baking soda. Use 2 on/off turns to combine. Add the flour and cranberries and use 2 on/off turns to combine.

Pour the batter evenly into 6 buttered standard muffin cups or 3 buttered 6-ounce custard cups. Bake in the preheated oven for 25 to 30 minutes. Serve warm.

HAM & CHEESE MUFFINS

These muffins are equally good to eat for breakfast or supper.

Makes 6 standard muffins or 3 mega-muffins

Preheat the oven to 350 degrees

1 ounce ham, cut into pieces

1 ounce sharp cheddar cheese, cut into pieces

2 tablespoons butter

1 egg

½ cup milk

1 teaspoon baking powder

1 cup flour

¼ teaspoon salt

Insert the chopping blade and add the ham and cheese. Use 10 to 12 on/off turns until chopped. Set aside.

Place the butter and egg in the work bowl and use 6 to 8 on/off turns until well combined. Add the milk and baking powder and use 2 on/off turns to combine. Add the flour, salt, and the reserved ham-and-cheese mixture and use 2 on/off turns to combine.

Pour the batter evenly into 6 buttered standard muffin cups or 3 buttered 6-ounce custard cups. Bake in the preheated oven for 25 to 30 minutes. Serve warm.

LEMON LOAF

This quickly made fragrant lemon bread is good on its own, spread with sweet butter, or used to make an avocado sandwich! A vegetable peeler removes the rind from a fresh lemon without picking up any of the bitter white pith, and combining the rind with the sugar in the recipe makes it easy to grate in the mini processor.

Makes one 5-by-2-inch loaf

Preheat the oven to 350 degrees

⅓ **cup sugar**

Rind of ½ lemon

3 tablespoons butter, cut into pieces

1 egg

¼ **cup fresh lemon juice**

½ **teaspoon baking powder**

¼ **teaspoon baking soda**

¾ **cup flour**

½ **teaspoon poppy seeds**

Insert the chopping blade, add the sugar and lemon rind and process until finely minced. Add the butter and cream it, using 6 to 8 on/off turns. Add the egg and lemon juice and use 4 to 6 on/off turns to combine. Add the baking powder and baking soda and use 2 on/off turns to blend. Add the flour and poppy seeds and use 2 on/off turns until just combined. Do not overprocess (traces of flour may be visible)!

Transfer the batter to a buttered mini-loaf pan. Bake in the preheated oven for 35 to 40 minutes until the bread begins to shrink from the sides of the pan.

Cool for 10 minutes on a rack before turning out of the pan.

POPOVERS

It's hard to top popovers straight out of the oven! A word of warning, though. Even if you fear the house is burning down, resist the temptation to peek in the oven or the cooler air will prevent the popovers from rising to their full potential. You can make a cheese variation by putting 1 ounce of a hard cheese, cut into pieces, into the work bowl and using 10 to 12 on/off turns to chop the cheese into tiny pieces. Continue with the recipe as directed.

Makes 6 popovers

Preheat the oven to 450 degrees

2 eggs

1 cup milk

1 tablespoon butter, melted and cooled, or 1 tablespoon vegetable oil

1 cup flour

Pinch salt

Insert the chopping blade and add the eggs, milk, and butter. Use 2 on/off turns to combine. Add the flour and salt and use 2 more on/off turns until just combined. Do not overprocess.

Pour the batter evenly about three-quarters of the way up 6 buttered standard muffin cups.

Bake in the preheated oven for 20 minutes. Without opening the oven door, lower the temperature to 350 degrees and bake for an additional 25 minutes. If you would like the centers a little firmer, pierce the popovers with a fork to allow the steam to escape and bake for another 5 minutes. Serve piping hot.

OUR LABOR AND OUR GOODS ARE FIGHTING

Salads & Vegetables

CAULIFLOWER MOUSSE

Unless you taste this, you cannot begin to imagine how good it is. It has an extraordinary creaminess, and its soft smooth texture makes it a splendid accompaniment for sliced roast meats.

Serves 2–3

**½ medium-size head cauliflower,
cut into florets**

2 tablespoons butter

1 tablespoon flour

½ cup milk

½ teaspoon salt

Pinch nutmeg

Freshly ground pepper

Blanch the cauliflower in a pot of boiling water for 10 minutes or until soft and tender. Drain well.

Meanwhile, heat 1 tablespoon of the butter in a small saucepan. Stir in the flour and then add the milk gradually, stirring with a whisk to form a smooth sauce. Season with the salt, the nutmeg, and pepper to taste.

Pour the sauce into the work bowl with the chopping blade inserted. Add the cauliflower and process until smooth. Heat the remaining tablespoon of butter in a small skillet and add the cauliflower mousse. Stir over low heat until very hot and serve.

COLESLAW

No matter how sophisticated we think we are, coleslaw is among our longtime favorite foods. Coleslaw can elevate a hot dog into a thing of beauty!

Makes 4 cups

2 medium-size carrots, peeled

1 head cabbage, about 1 pound, cored and halved

½ small onion

½ medium-size green pepper, seeded and quartered

¾ cup Mayonnaise (page 72)

¼ cup sour cream

¼ cup milk

2 tablespoons vinegar

½ teaspoon celery seeds

Cut the carrots into even lengths to fit the feed tube. Insert the shredding disc, stand the carrots upright in the feed tube, and shred, using medium pressure. Set aside in a mixing bowl.

Cut each cabbage half into 8 wedges. Insert the chopping blade and fill the work bowl no more than half full. Use 4 to 8 on/off turns to chop the cabbage to the size you like. Add to the carrot in the mixing bowl. Repeat with the remaining cabbage. Add the onion to the work bowl and use 3 on/off turns to chop. Add to the cabbage.

Place the remaining ingredients except the celery seed in the work bowl. Use 4 to 6 on/off turns to combine the dressing and chop the green pepper. Add to the mixing bowl with the celery seed and stir to combine. Chill until serving time.

CUCUMBER SALAD

This salad has a refreshing flavor and a satisfying crunch!

Serves 6

2 medium-size cucumbers, peeled and halved lengthwise

1 medium-size onion, halved

8 medium-size radishes, trimmed

1 cup sour cream

3 tablespoons white vinegar

3 tablespoons vegetable oil

¼ teaspoon paprika

Salt and pepper to taste

Cut the cucumbers in pieces to fit the feed tube. Insert the slicing disc and place 2 cucumber pieces in the feed tube. Slice, using medium pressure. Repeat until all of the cucumbers are sliced. Slice the onion halves and radishes in the same manner. Empty the work bowl as needed into a large mixing bowl.

Insert the chopping blade, add the remaining ingredients, and use on/off turns to combine. Pour the dressing over the vegetables and mix well. Chill for at least 1 hour.

POTATOES AU GRATIN

Serve this dish with a nice broiled or roast chicken and a fresh steamed vegetable and you will have a splendid supper.

Serves 2–3

Preheat the oven to 350 degrees

2 ounces cheddar cheese

1 large baking potato, peeled and quartered

½ medium-size onion

1 cup heavy cream

Salt and white pepper

Insert the shredding disc and place the cheese in the feed tube. Use medium pressure to shred. Set aside.

Insert the slicing disc and slice the potato quarters, using medium pressure. Slice the onion in the same manner. Place half of the potatoes and onion in a 1-quart buttered casserole. Pour ½ cup of the cream on top. Season with salt and pepper and sprinkle with half of the cheese. Layer with the remaining potatoes and onion, pour the remaining cream on top, and sprinkle with the remaining cheese. Bake in the preheated oven for 40 to 50 minutes or until the potatoes are tender.

PUREED VEGETABLES

This simplest of vegetable dishes is also one of the tastiest. The best vegetables to puree are starchy ones such as the root vegetables, or winter squashes, or a combination. Choose from parsnips, turnips, carrots, rutabaga, potatoes, yams, celery root, acorn squash, or beets. For example, a medium-size rutabaga and a large carrot combine to produce a beautiful color, texture, and taste.

Serves 2–3

3 cups sliced vegetables (see below)

2–3 tablespoons butter, room temperature

Salt and pepper

Peel and trim the vegetables, then cut in pieces to fit the feed tube. Insert the slicing disc and place the vegetable pieces in the feed tube. Slice, using medium pressure.

Place the vegetables in a saucepan. Add sufficient water to cover, then cover the pan and cook for 20 to 30 minutes or until tender. Drain well and return them to the heat for about a minute, stirring with a wooden spoon in order to evaporate any excess moisture.

Insert the chopping blade in the work bowl and add the hot vegetables. Use 10 to 12 on/off turns to chop. Add the butter and process until smooth. Season with salt and pepper and serve. You may make this in advance and refrigerate. Reheat in the microwave for 3 or 4 minutes just before serving, or cover the dish with aluminum foil and put it in a preheated 350-degree oven for about 12 minutes.

SAUTÉED RED CABBAGE

Here's a traditional Pennsylvania Dutch side dish that goes well with pork.

Serves 4

1 head red cabbage, about 1 pound, halved and cored

1 small onion, quartered

2 tablespoons butter

1 cup unsweetened apple juice or cider

2 tablespoons vinegar

1 teaspoon caraway seeds

Salt and pepper

Cut each cabbage half into 8 pieces. Insert the chopping blade and fill the work bowl no more than half full. Use 4 to 8 on/off turns to chop the cabbage to the size you like. Set aside in a mixing bowl. Repeat with the remaining cabbage. Add the onion to the work bowl and use 3 on/off turns to chop.

Heat the butter in a large skillet and add the cabbage and onion. Cook, stirring, for 3 to 4 minutes. Add the apple juice and vinegar, cover, and simmer until tender, about 10 to 15 minutes. Stir in the caraway seeds, season to taste with salt and pepper, and serve.

SPINACH & ARTICHOKE AU GRATIN

This is one of those important dishes that round out a meal with more flair than brussels sprouts can ever muster.

Serves 4

Preheat the oven to 350 degrees

¾ pound spinach, washed and stems removed

1 slice bread, lightly buttered and cut in quarters

1 clove garlic

Leaves of 1 sprig fresh oregano

3 ounces cream cheese

¼ cup milk

2 cooked artichoke hearts, quartered

Cook the spinach in a large saucepan over moderate heat, with only the water clinging to the leaves, for 3 to 5 minutes or until the leaves are just wilted; drain well.

Insert the chopping blade and add the bread. Use on/off turns until it has turned to crumbs; set aside. Add the garlic to the work bowl and use on/off turns until finely minced. Add the oregano and use on/off turns until finely minced. Add the cream cheese and milk. Use 6 to 8 on/off turns until well combined and creamy.

Place the drained spinach in a buttered 1-quart casserole. Arrange the artichoke quarters over the spinach, cover with the cream sauce, and sprinkle with the bread crumbs. Bake for 12 minutes or until heated through and the crumbs are toasted.

STIR-FRIED VEGETABLES

One of the very best uses of the mini processor is for cutting and slicing vegetables. The mighty little machine will eliminate hours spent at this chore.

Serves 4

1 clove garlic

½ small onion

½ medium-size green or red pepper, seeded

1 small, slender zucchini

6 medium-size mushrooms, stems removed

1 medium-size carrot, peeled

2 tablespoons vegetable or peanut oil

4 ounces snow peas, trimmed

Soy sauce (optional)

Sesame oil (optional)

Insert the chopping blade and add the garlic. Use on/off turns until finely minced.

Insert the slicing blade and place the onion half in the feed tube. Slice, using medium pressure. Set the garlic and onion aside. Even the bottom of the pepper, place it cut side down in the feed tube, and slice, using light pressure; set aside. Cut the zucchini in lengths to fit the feed tube. Place the pieces side by side in the tube and slice, using medium pressure. Stack the mushrooms on their sides in the feed tube and slice, using light pressure. Set the zucchini and mushrooms aside.

Insert the shredding disc. Cut the carrot in lengths to fit the feed tube horizontally and shred the carrot pieces on the horizontal.

Heat 1 tablespoon of the oil in a wok or large skillet over medium-high heat. Add the garlic and onion and stir-fry until the onions have just wilted. Add the green pepper and stir-fry until just softened. Add the zucchini and the mushrooms and stir-fry until the zucchini is a very bright green. Add the remaining oil as needed. Add the carrots and snow peas and stir-fry just until the snow peas are bright green. Season with soy sauce and a dash of sesame oil if desired. Serve immediately.

STUFFED
GREEN PEPPERS

This meal-in-one has many variations. For example, you can substitute chicken for the beef and add a few slices of mushroom or other vegetable to the stuffing mixture.

Serves 2

Preheat the oven to 350 degrees

2 medium-size green peppers

1 clove garlic

½ small onion, cut in pieces

½ pound lean ground beef

½ cup cooked rice

8 ounces Tomato Sauce (page 71)

2 ounces cheddar cheese

Cut a thin slice from the stem end of each pepper, discard the stem, and reserve the pieces of green pepper from this slice.

Hollow out the shells of the peppers, discarding the seeds and ribs. Simmer the peppers for 5 minutes in enough boiling water to cover, then drain. Set aside.

Insert the chopping blade in the work bowl and add the garlic. Use on/off turns until finely minced. Add the onion and reserved green pepper pieces. Use 3 to 4 on/off turns to chop.

Fry the beef with the garlic, onion, and pepper in a small skillet over moderate heat until the beef is browned and the vegetables have softened. Drain off the excess fat. Stir in the rice and half of the tomato sauce. Lightly stuff the peppers and set them upright in a 1-quart casserole. Spoon any remaining meat mixture around the filled peppers. Pour the remaining tomato sauce over the top.

Insert the shredding disc. Place the cheese in the feed tube and shred, using light pressure. Sprinkle the cheese on top of the peppers and meat mixture. Cover the casserole and bake for 35 to 40 minutes. Uncover and bake for an additional 10 minutes or until the cheese is brown and bubbling and the peppers are tender.

STUFFED TOMATOES

Everything from herbed bread crumbs to chopped chicken can be used for stuffing tomatoes. This recipe uses a vegetable salad, making it a lovely summer side dish.

Serves 6

6 medium-size fresh, ripe tomatoes

1 ½ teaspoons salt, plus more to taste

Freshly ground black pepper

1 medium-size carrot, peeled and cut in 4 even lengths

1 small potato, peeled and quartered

½ cup freshly shelled peas

8 sprigs parsley

2 small scallions, cut in pieces

1 hard-cooked egg, halved

⅓ cup Mayonnaise (page 72)

3 black olives, pitted and halved

Cut a slice from the stem end of each tomato. Scoop out the tomato pulp. Discard the seeds and set the pulp aside. Sprinkle the shells with the 1 ½ teaspoons salt and pepper to taste. Invert on a wire rack and leave to drain for 15 minutes.

Insert the slicing disc in the work bowl and place the carrot lengths in the feed tube. Slice, using medium pressure. Place a potato quarter cut side down in the feed tube and slice, using medium pressure. Continue with the remaining quarters. Cook the carrot and potato slices in a pot of boiling salted water until just tender, about 10 minutes; drain well. Cook the peas in the boiling water for about 1 to 2 minutes; drain well. Chill the vegetables while you prepare the remaining ingredients.

Wipe the work bowl dry and insert the chopping blade. Add the parsley and use on/off turns until minced. Add the scallions and use on/off turns until chopped. Set both aside. Add the egg and use 2 on/off turns to chop. Set aside.

Add the reserved tomato pulp to the work bowl and use 6 to 8 on/off turns to chop. Combine with the chilled vegetables, the chopped parsley and scallions, and the mayonnaise; stir well. Season with salt and pepper to taste. Fill the tomato shells with the mixture and garnish with the chopped egg and the olive halves.

SWEET POTATO CRISP

This dish will satisfy anyone's craving for a little something sweet, say, alongside the turkey at Thanksgiving.

Serves 4

Preheat the oven to 350 degrees

2–3 medium-size sweet potatoes, about 1 pound, peeled and sliced ⅜ inch thick

4 tablespoons butter, room temperature

2 tablespoons flour

¼ cup brown sugar

2 tablespoons milk or cream

¼ cup pecan halves

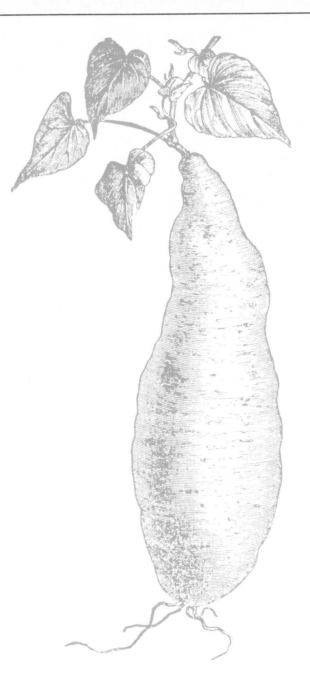

Place the potato slices in a medium-sized shallow baking dish. Cover and bake in the preheated oven for 15 minutes.

Preheat the broiler. Insert the chopping blade and add the remaining ingredients. Use 3 to 4 on/off turns to mix, then process until combined and the nuts are finely chopped. Spread the mixture over the hot potatoes. Broil for 5 to 7 minutes or until bubbly and caramelized.

SAUCES & DRESSINGS

CREAMY BLUE CHEESE DRESSING

This dressing is the perfect complement to a combination of greens plus sliced, tart apples and a sprinkle of walnuts. Calorie watchers may substitute low-fat cottage cheese for the cream cheese and plain yogurt for the sour cream.

Makes 2 cups

1 clove garlic

8 sprigs parsley

4 sprigs fresh chives

8 ounces cream cheese

½ cup sour cream

2 ounces blue cheese

2–4 tablespoons milk

Insert the chopping blade and add the garlic. Use on/off turns to process until minced. Add the parsley and chives and use on/off turns until minced. Add the cream cheese, sour cream, and blue cheese. Use 6 to 8 on/off turns to combine, then process until smooth. Add the milk through the opening in the work bowl cover to thin the dressing to the consistency you like. Chill before serving.

FRESH BASIL DRESSING

This dressing is the ultimate match for perfectly sliced, vine-ripened tomatoes and thin strips of fresh mozzarella. Or try it on your favorite pasta.

Makes 1 cup

1 clove garlic

8 fresh basil leaves

2 tablespoons white wine vinegar

2 tablespoons fresh lemon juice

½ cup vegetable oil

Salt and freshly ground pepper

Insert the chopping blade and add the garlic and basil. Use on/off turns until finely minced. With the machine on, pour the vinegar, lemon juice, and oil through the opening in the work bowl cover. Process until creamy and season with salt and pepper to taste.

FRESH TOMATO SAUCE

Use the ripest tomatoes you can find for this sauce, which can top any variety of pasta. Adding canned tomato paste may seem like an insult to their freshness, but, in fact, it gives a fine, intense boost of flavor and is the key ingredient that holds the sauce together.

Makes 1½ cups

2 cloves garlic

10–12 fresh basil leaves

½ small onion

1–2 tablespoons olive oil

6 plum tomatoes, halved and seeded

6 medium-size mushrooms, trimmed

2 teaspoons tomato paste

¼ teaspoon salt

¼ cup water

Insert the chopping blade and add the garlic and basil. Use on/off turns until minced. Add the onion and use 3 to 4 on/off turns to chop. Cook this mixture in 1 tablespoon olive oil in a small skillet until softened. Place the tomato halves in the work bowl and use on/off turns to chop to the consistency you like. Set aside.

Insert the slicing disc and place the mushrooms on their sides in the feed tube. Slice, using light pressure. Add the mushrooms to the skillet along with the additional oil if needed. Cook until softened. Add the chopped tomatoes, tomato paste, salt, and water and stir well to combine. Heat until thoroughly warm.

Serve over ½ pound freshly cooked pasta. Pass a bowl of freshly grated Parmesan, Romano, or Kasseri cheese at the table.

MAYONNAISE

If you think it prudent, you may decide to replace the whole egg in this recipe with two egg whites for a lighter mayonnaise. It won't taste the same as real, rich, delectable mayonnaise, but life is full of small compromises.

Makes 1¼ cups

1 egg, or better yet, 2 egg yolks

1 tablespoon cider vinegar or fresh lemon juice

1 teaspoon Dijon mustard

Dash cayenne pepper

1 cup vegetable oil

Insert the chopping blade and add all of the ingredients except the oil. Use 2 on/off turns to blend. With the machine on, pour in the oil very slowly in a thin stream through the opening in the work bowl cover until the mixture is completely combined, thick, and creamy. This will keep, refrigerated, for up to 3 weeks.

MEXICAN SALSA

The burgeoning Mexican, Thai, Indian, and Vietnamese populations of the United States have brought the herb cilantro, which is fresh coriander, to the forefront of today's markets. It has a distinctive taste and here it combines with hot peppers in a spicy sauce to serve with tortilla chips, a Spanish omelet, or grilled meat. Remember to handle hot peppers carefully. Once you have cut them, do not touch any part of your face, and wash your hands with soap and water right away.

Makes 1½ cups

1 clove garlic

1 small jalapeño or serrano pepper, seeded

1½ teaspoons fresh oregano leaves

1 scallion, cut in pieces

¼ cup cilantro leaves

4 plum tomatoes

1½ tablespoons vinegar

2 teaspoons olive oil

Insert the chopping blade and add the garlic, pepper, and oregano. Use on/off turns until very finely minced. Add the scallion and cilantro and use 4 to 6 on/off turns to chop. Add the remaining ingredients and use 3 to 4 on/off turns to chop the tomatoes and combine the ingredients. The texture should be coarse.

OIL & VINEGAR DRESSING

I like the small amount of sugar in here to take some of the "bite" out of the dressing, but you can omit it if you prefer.

Makes 1 cup

2 cloves garlic

2 teaspoons Dijon mustard

¼ cup red wine vinegar

¾ cup olive oil

½ teaspoon sugar

¼ teaspoon salt

Freshly ground pepper

Insert the chopping blade and add the garlic. Use on/off turns until finely minced. While the machine is on, pour the remaining ingredients through the opening in the work bowl cover. Process until creamy.

PARMESAN CREAM SAUCE

Here is a fast sauce that can be made while the pasta cooks. For variation, add shrimp or small pieces of ham to the garlic, fry briefly, then proceed. Or try this sauce over cooked vegetables.

Makes about 1 cup

4 ounces Parmesan cheese, cut in ½-inch cubes

10–12 sprigs parsley

2 cloves garlic

1 tablespoon butter

¾ cup heavy cream

Salt and pepper

Insert the chopping blade and add the cheese. Use on/off turns to chop, then process until finely grated; set aside. Add the parsley, use on/off turns to chop, and set aside.

Add the garlic to the work bowl and use on/off turns until minced. Heat the butter in a medium-sized skillet and add the garlic. Cook until softened but not browned. Add the cream and heat through. Season to taste with salt and pepper.

Pour the sauce over 1 pound of freshly cooked pasta and add the reserved parsley and half the cheese. Toss well to coat. Adjust the seasonings and serve, sprinkled with additional cheese.

PESTO

If fresh basil is in short supply, substitute young spinach leaves and add dried basil. You can do a lot with pesto besides serving it on pasta. Substitute ⅓ cup mayonnaise for the oil in this recipe, spread the pesto on sliced baguettes, and broil until bubbly and lightly browned. Or try adding dollops of pesto to pizza during the last two minutes of cooking time.

Makes 1 cup

2 ounces Parmesan cheese, cut into pieces

1 clove garlic

1½ cups packed basil leaves (about 2 bunches)

½ cup pine nuts or walnuts

¼ teaspoon salt

⅓ cup olive oil

Insert the chopping blade and add the cheese. Use on/off turns to process until finely grated. Set aside.

Add the garlic to the work bowl and use on/off turns until minced. Add the basil, nuts, and salt and use 8 to 10 on/off turns to chop coarsely. Add the cheese, and with the machine on, pour the oil through the opening in the work bowl cover. Process until smooth.

Store in the refrigerator in a covered jar with 1 tablespoon olive oil on the surface to prevent the pesto from darkening. Stir the oil into the pesto before serving. Or freeze, and stir in the oil after the pesto has thawed.

SPECIAL SAUCE
FOR ARTICHOKES

*Invite your best friends over and provide each with one whole artichoke,
a plate on which to put the leaves, and a small pot of this sauce.
What more does anyone need?*

Makes 1 cup

1 hard-cooked egg, halved

¼ cup parsley leaves

3 scallions, cut in pieces

1 clove garlic

1½ tablespoons capers

3 sweet gherkins

2 tablespoons red wine vinegar

½ teaspoon Dijon mustard

Pinch salt

Freshly ground pepper

¼ cup light olive oil

Insert the chopping blade and add the egg. Use on/off turns until finely chopped; set aside.

Add the parsley, scallions, and garlic to the work bowl and use on/off turns until minced. Add the capers and gherkins and use on/off turns until finely chopped. Add the vinegar, mustard, salt, and pepper to taste and use on/off turns to combine.

With the machine on, slowly pour the oil through the opening in the work bowl cover and process until creamy. Add the chopped egg and use on/off turns until just combined.

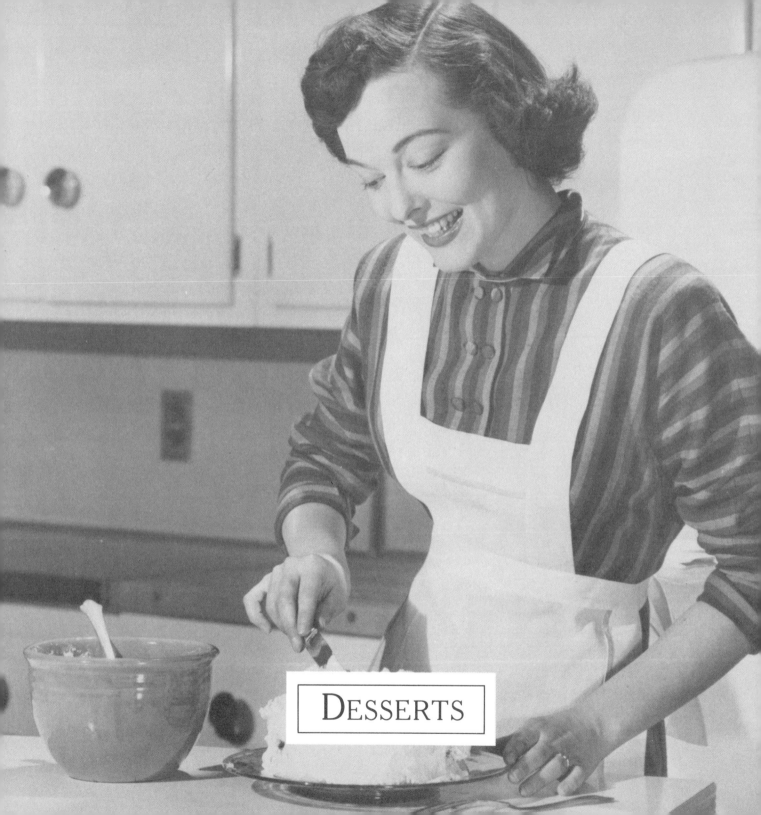

DESSERTS

ALMOND-COCONUT SQUARES

Here is a moist, rich treat, with a texture somewhere between a bar cookie and a cake. When baked in a larger pan, the results are bar-like squares, while baking in a smaller pan gives greater depth and the lightness of a cake.

Makes 16 squares

Preheat the oven to 325 degrees

¼ cup blanched almonds

¼ cup brown sugar

½ cup shredded, unsweetened coconut

8 tablespoons butter, cut in pieces

2 eggs

1 cup sugar

1 teaspoon almond extract

1 cup flour

Insert the chopping blade and add the almonds, brown sugar, and half of the coconut. Use 4 to 6 on/off turns to chop the nuts and combine the ingredients. Set aside.

Add the butter, eggs, sugar, and almond flavoring to the work bowl. Use on/off turns to process until the mixture is smooth and creamy. Add the flour and the remaining coconut and use 3 on/off turns to combine. Spread the batter in an 8- or 9-inch-square baking pan and sprinkle the reserved almond mixture over the top. Press the topping lightly into the batter. Bake for 30 to 35 minutes in the preheated oven or until a toothpick comes out dry (there may be a few crumbs).

Cool in the pan on a rack, then cut into 16 squares.

Chocolate Chip Cookies

What could be more worth raiding the kitchen for than chocolate chip cookies?

Makes 1½ dozen

Preheat the oven to 375 degrees

8 tablespoons cold butter, cut in pieces

¼ cup brown sugar

¼ cup sugar

1 egg

½ teaspoon baking soda

1 teaspoon vanilla extract

Pinch salt

1 cup flour

½ cup semisweet chocolate chips

Insert the chopping blade and add the butter and the brown and the white sugars. Use 4 to 6 on/off turns to blend. Add the egg, baking soda, vanilla, and salt and process until smooth and creamy. Add the flour and use 3 on/off turns to combine. Remove the chopping blade and stir the chocolate chips into the batter. Drop by tablespoonfuls onto an ungreased baking sheet. Bake for 6 to 8 minutes or until just golden on the bottoms. Cool the cookies slightly on the baking sheets before transferring them to a rack to cool completely.

LEMON COOKIES

Rolling the dough in sugar gives these cookies a shiny glazed appearance. Try serving them with the Fresh Fruit Sorbet (page 92).

Makes approximately 30 cookies

Preheat the oven to 400 degrees

Rind of ½ lemon

⅓ cup sugar, plus more for rolling the dough in

1 egg

6 tablespoons butter, cut in pieces

1 cup flour

Insert the chopping blade into the work bowl and add the lemon rind and the ⅓ cup sugar. Use on/off turns until the rind is finely chopped. Add the egg and butter and use 4 to 6 on/off turns until the butter is chopped. Process for 10 to 15 seconds until smooth. Add the flour and use 3 on/off turns to combine. Chill the dough for 1 hour or until you can shape it.

Form the dough into 1-inch balls, roll them in the additional sugar and place on ungreased baking sheets 2 inches apart. Flatten with the bottom of a glass. Bake for 6 minutes until the tops are shiny and the edges are lightly golden brown.

PECAN LAYER BARS

It takes less than five minutes to make homemade cookies in the mini processor. You could, if you were feeling generous, take a gift of cookies to a friend.

Makes 16 squares

Preheat the oven to 350 degrees

6 tablespoons butter, cut in pieces

6 tablespoons confectioners' sugar

¾ cup plus 1 tablespoon flour

1 egg

½ cup brown sugar

¼ teaspoon baking powder

½ teaspoon vanilla extract

½ cup pecan halves

Insert the chopping blade and add the butter, confectioners' sugar, and the ¾ cup flour. Use 8 to 10 on/off turns until the mixture resembles coarse meal. Press lightly into an 8-inch-square baking pan. Bake for 10 to 12 minutes.

Prepare the second layer while the crust is baking. Add the remaining 1 tablespoon flour and then the remaining ingredients to the work bowl. Use 3 to 5 on/off turns to combine and chop the pecans coarsely. Spread this mixture over the warm crust and continue baking for another 15 minutes. Cool and then cut into bars.

Apple-Cinnamon Sauce

As apples are always available, so should there be a permanent supply of homemade applesauce in the refrigerator. In season, you could substitute pears or peaches.

Makes 1 cup

2-3 small cooking apples (such as Golden Delicious), peeled, halved, and cored

¼ cup sugar

½ cup water

⅛ teaspoon cinnamon

Pinch nutmeg

2 teaspoons cornstarch

Slice a thin slice off the stem end of the apple halves. Insert the slicing disc and the cover and place the apple halves, flat end down, in the feed tube. Insert the pusher and use medium pressure to slice. Continue with the remaining apples. Measure out 2 to 2½ cups.

Place the apples in a saucepan with the sugar and ¼ cup of the water, bring to a boil and then reduce to a simmer. Cover and cook for 10 minutes or until tender. Combine the spices and cornstarch with the remaining ¼ cup water. Stir this mixture into the apples, bring to a boil, and cook 1 minute. Serve warm over ice cream or pound cake or as a side dish with pork or poultry.

Butterscotch Sauce

You'll want to make two batches of this recipe in order to have enough on hand for late-night indulgences. Keep it refrigerated and then reheat before serving. The fastest way to make a hot butterscotch sauce is to reheat it in the microwave oven. But be careful—the microwaves are attracted to the sugar and if you try to swallow it too quickly, it will tear out the roof of your mouth!

Makes 1 cup

1 cup butterscotch chips

⅓ cup milk

4 tablespoons butter

1 teaspoon vanilla extract, brandy, or rum

Insert the chopping blade and add the butterscotch chips. Use on/off turns until the chips are coarsely chopped. Heat the milk and butter in a saucepan until very hot. Pour the mixture onto the butterscotch through the opening in the top of the work bowl. Process until smooth. Add the vanilla or other flavoring and process until blended. Serve warm over ice cream.

Hot Fudge Sauce

Serve this sauce with the Dessert Crêpes (page 91) and your favorite ice cream.

Makes about 2 cups

3 ounces best-quality unsweetened chocolate, cut in pieces

1 cup sugar

½ cup cream

4 tablespoons butter

1 teaspoon vanilla extract

Dash salt

Insert the chopping blade into the work bowl and add the chocolate and sugar. Use 8 to 10 on/off turns to chop, then process for about 2 minutes to chop the chocolate almost as finely as the sugar. Heat the cream and butter in a saucepan until very warm and then pour the mixture through the opening in the work bowl cover while the machine is turned on. Process until smooth. Add the vanilla and salt and use on/off turns to combine. For an even thicker sauce, cook in a saucepan over medium-low heat for an additional 10 minutes. Serve warm. You may store this sauce in the refrigerator and simply reheat it before using.

CHEESECAKE WITH GRAHAM CRACKER CRUST

Another task perfectly suited to the mini processor is grinding graham crackers to make a crumb crust. And this sour cream-topped-cheesecake is just the right thing to put in it.

Makes one 8- or 9-inch pie

Preheat the oven to 350 degrees

CRUST	FILLING	TOPPING
12 graham cracker squares	11 ounces cream cheese, cut into 12 pieces	⅔ cup sour cream
2 tablespoons sugar	2 eggs	2 tablespoons sugar
2 tablespoons butter	⅓ cup sugar	½ teaspoon vanilla extract
	1 teaspoon vanilla extract	

For the crust, insert the chopping blade into the work bowl and add the graham crackers. Use 4 to 6 on/off turns to chop. Add the sugar and butter and use on/off turns until well combined. Press into an 8- or 9-inch pie plate. Bake in the preheated oven for 6 to 8 minutes or until lightly golden brown.

For the filling, add the cream cheese, eggs, sugar, and vanilla to the work bowl. Use 4 to 6 on/off turns to combine, scrape down the work bowl, and continue to process until smooth. Pour the filling into the baked pie shell and bake in the preheated oven for 25 to 35 minutes until puffy and lightly golden brown. Cool on a rack for 15 minutes.

For the topping, stir together all of the ingredients and spread over the warm cheesecake. Bake for an additional 10 minutes at 350 degrees, covering the edge of the pan with foil if the crust is browning too much. Cool on a rack and then chill until serving time.

CHOCOLATE MOUSSE

There are thousands of recipes for chocolate mousse. This, with its hint of orange, is our favorite version. I keep it frozen, too, as solace for life's little problems.

Serves 4

¾ cup heavy cream

1 egg, separated

3 ounces best-quality bittersweet chocolate, cut in pieces, or ½ cup semisweet chocolate chips

2 tablespoons sugar

1 tablespoon cocoa

3 tablespoons butter

1 tablespoon liqueur, such as Grand Marnier, Truffles Liqueur du Chocolat, or Frangelico (optional)

Insert the chopping blade and add the heavy cream and the egg white. Process until the cream thickens and becomes stiff. Set aside.

Place the chocolate, sugar, and cocoa in the work bowl. Use on/off turns to chop the chocolate finely. Heat the butter until hot but do not let it brown. Pour the butter through the opening in the top of the work bowl with the machine turned on and process until smooth. Add the egg yolk and liqueur and use 3 to 5 on/off turns to combine. Add the whipped cream and use 2 to 4 on/off turns until the cream has just blended with the chocolate. Pour into 4 individual serving dishes. Chill before serving.

Top with a fresh or candied violet or any other fanciful decoration.

DESSERT CRÊPES

*Crêpes have stepped right back into fashion again. Invest in a special
crêpe pan or small, shallow non-stick skillet to be sure of the best results.*

Makes 1 dozen crêpes

2 eggs

⅔ cup flour

⅔ cup water

1 tablespoon butter, melted and cooled

¼ teaspoon salt

½ teaspoon sugar

Vegetable oil or butter, for the pan

Insert the chopping blade and add the eggs. Use 3 on/off turns to beat them. Add the remaining ingredients and process for 5 to 10 seconds to mix until smooth. Refrigerate for 30 minutes to an hour.

Heat a crêpe pan or 8-inch skillet over moderate heat and brush lightly with vegetable oil or butter. Pour approximately 3 tablespoons of the batter into the center of the pan and tilt the pan to spread the batter evenly and quickly over the bottom. Tip out any excess batter.

Cook for almost 1 minute or until the edges begin to brown and the batter has lost its shine. Turn the crêpe onto the other side and cook for 30 seconds until lightly browned, then slide it onto a plate. Continue with the remaining batter, oiling the pan only when necessary.

Stack the cooked crêpes on top of one another and keep warm in a very low oven. Serve warm, filled with ice cream and topped with Apple-Cinnamon Sauce (page 85) or Hot Fudge Sauce (page 86).

FRESH FRUIT
SORBETS

I beg your indulgence in allowing me to declare that the only *way to make a glorious sorbet is to select the most gloriously fresh fruit at its peak of juicy ripeness. To intensify the taste of the sorbet, you may want to add a tablespoon of fruit brandy to the mixture. Beware the temptation to add more than a tiny taste or the alcohol will prevent it from freezing firmly.*

Serves 2
(or perhaps 1 if you are watching a long movie)

1 ½ cups fresh berries or thinly sliced peaches, nectarines, or other fruit, or substitute passion fruit pulp or juice

¼ cup unsweetened orange, apple, or other fruit juice

1 tablespoon sugar (optional)

1 tablespoon pear, raspberry, or other fruit brandy (optional)

Insert the chopping blade and add all of the ingredients. Process until the mixture is smooth. If you have decided to make a berry sorbet, you may want to strain the mixture to remove the tiny seeds.

Pour the mixture into a Donvier or other ice cream maker and freeze according to the manufacturer's directions until firm. This will take anywhere from 20 minutes for the Donvier or a similar type of ice cream maker to an hour or so for other manufacturers' models.

If you do not have any kind of ice cream maker, do not despair. Pour the mixture into a bowl and put it into the freezer. Beat the sorbet with a wooden spoon every 30 minutes to prevent ice crystals from forming.

One-Crust
Pastry Shell

*There are few greater achievements to aspire to than the ability to bake
your own pie. Let the processor do the work. You can take the credit.*

Makes one 8- or 9-inch pie shell

Preheat the oven to 425 degrees

1 ¼ cups flour

½ teaspoon salt

4 tablespoons cold butter

2 tablespoons vegetable shortening

3 tablespoons ice water

Insert the chopping blade and add the flour, salt, butter, and vegetable shortening. Use 10 to 12 on/off turns to blend to a coarse meal consistency. Add the water through the opening in the work bowl cover and process for about 10 seconds or until the dough begins to come together but is still crumbly. Do not overprocess. Place the mixture in plastic wrap and press together to form into a disc. Chill for 15 minutes, if desired, before rolling out.

Roll out the pastry on a lightly floured surface and fit it into a pie plate. Trim the edges and form a rim. Prick the crust all over with a fork to allow the air to escape. Line it with foil or wax paper and weight it down with dried beans, rice, or pastry weights.

Bake the prepared shell for 10 minutes, then remove the foil or wax paper and the weights. Bake an additional 8 to 10 minutes or until browned.

PUMPKIN CHIFFON PIE

Crystallized ginger can be found among the jars of spices in specialty food stores or the supermarket. The pumpkin chiffon also tastes very good on its own, spooned into sherbet glasses and served as a mousse.

Makes one 8- or 9-inch pie

PUMPKIN FILLING

⅓ cup brown sugar

1 tablespoon crystallized ginger

1¼ cups cooked pumpkin,
fresh or canned

1 envelope unflavored gelatin

3 egg yolks

½ teaspoon cinnamon

¼ teaspoon salt

¼ teaspoon nutmeg

CHIFFON FILLING

3 egg whites

¼ teaspoon salt

¼ teaspoon cream of tartar

6 tablespoons sugar

One 8- or 9-inch baked Pastry Shell
(page 94)
Whipped cream and slivers of
crystallized ginger, for decoration

For the pumpkin filling, insert the chopping blade and add the brown sugar and crystallized ginger. Use on/off turns until chopped. Combine with all of the pumpkin filling ingredients in a large saucepan. Cook over moderate heat and bring to a boil. Remove from the heat and cool until the mixture mounds when dropped from a spoon. It will thicken as it cools. If the mixture gets too stiff, just whirl it in the mini processor for a few seconds before blending in the chiffon filling.

For the chiffon filling, place the egg whites in a clean straight-sided bowl with the salt and cream of tartar. Beat until foamy and add the sugar gradually. Continue beating until shiny and the meringue will hold stiff peaks. Fold the meringue into the pumpkin filling and spread evenly in the pie shell. Chill for a few hours until firm. Decorate with freshly whipped cream and slivers of crystallized ginger.

INDEX